Farm to Table

Seafood

ANN O. SQUIRE

Children's Press®
An Imprint of Scholastic Inc.

Content Consultant
Anuradha Prakash, PhD
Professor, Director, Food Science Program
Chapman University
Orange, California

Library of Congress Cataloging-in-Publication Data
Names: Squire, Ann, author.
Title: Seafood / by Ann O. Squire.
Other titles: True book.
Description: New York, NY : Children's Press, an imprint of Scholastic Inc., 2017. | Series: A true
  book | Includes bibliographical references and index.
Identifiers: LCCN 2016026974| ISBN 9780531229354 (library binding : alk. paper) | ISBN
  9780531235546 (pbk. : alk. paper)
Subjects: LCSH: Seafood—Juvenile literature. | Fish trade—Juvenile literature. | Fisheries—
  Juvenile literature. | Fish culture—Juvenile literature.
Classification: LCC SH327.5 .S68 2017 | DDC 338.3/727—dc23

Front cover: A diver catching a lobster
Back cover: A child with a fish he caught

Find the Truth!

Everything you are about to read is true *except* for one of the sentences on this page.

Which one is **TRUE**?

T or F   All fish live on a plant-based diet.

T or F   Fishers catch octopuses and eels using traps.

Find the answers in this book.

Contents

THE **BIG** TRUTH!

Running Out

Atlantic salmon

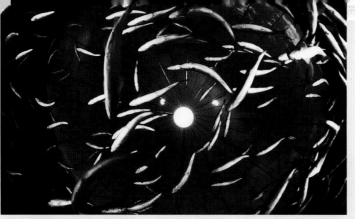

Salmon in a fish farm pen

Lobsters

From Ocean to Table

1 Fishing vessels set out.

2 Crew members release lines, nets, or other fishing gear. After a time, they pull the gear back in, bringing animals along with it.

From Hatchery to Table

2 When the hatched fish are big enough, they are transported to fish farms. Fish farms may also obtain some young fish or shellfish from the wild.

1 Hatcheries breed adult fish or shellfish and raise the animals' eggs.

4 Fish and shellfish are packaged and sold either fresh or frozen to grocery stores, restaurants, and other buyers. Some fishers sell directly to individuals.

3 Larger ships process and freeze their catch on board and spend weeks or months at sea. Smaller boats store their catch fresh and return to port the same day.

4 When the fish or shellfish are large enough, they are harvested, processed, and sold frozen or fresh.

3 The animals are raised in enclosures on land, in the water near land, or in the open ocean.

Many restaurants offer a variety of seafood choices from around the world.

CHAPTER 1

Where Does Your Seafood Come From?

It was Jane's birthday. To celebrate, Jane and her family went out to their favorite restaurant, a seafood place near the harbor. The restaurant had a big menu, so they all could order exactly what they wanted. Jane's mom ordered the special of the day, Chilean sea bass. Jane chose the broiled salmon, and her dad decided on the fresh, local lobster.

There are more than 27,000 identified species of fish on Earth.

Fish From Far and Near

Though the family didn't know it, the three fish they ordered came from very different places. The sea bass had lived in the cold waters near Antarctica. Fishing boats caught it using longlines, a length of fishing line with a series of baited hooks attached. The boats spent several weeks at sea, and the fish was stored frozen on the boat. When the boats reached port, the fish was shipped to markets thousands of miles away.

The Chilean sea bass is also called the Patagonian toothfish

Salmon swim in a fish farm pen in Canada.

Jane's salmon began its life not in the wild, but on a fish farm off the coast of eastern Canada. Fish farms breed fish and raise them in large tanks or enclosures. Enclosures often consist of cages or pens that are submerged, or kept underwater, away from the shore. A single pen may house thousands of fish. When the fish are big enough, they are harvested, processed, and sent to market.

Lobster claws are sharp and dangerous. Lobster handlers tie the claws closed so the animals cannot hurt people or other lobsters.

The lobster Jane's dad ordered had been caught nearby in the Atlantic Ocean. The fisher and his assistant used lobster traps. These traps are designed so lobsters can climb in but cannot climb out. The fishers collect and empty the traps each day before returning them to the water to catch more lobsters. After returning to the harbor at the end of each day, the crew delivered their catch directly to local markets and restaurants.

Who Eats Seafood?

Seafood is an excellent source of protein. This nutrient helps the body build and repair itself. Americans are among the world's top seafood consumers. Throughout Asia and Europe, seafood is a major part of the average diet. The same is true for Oceania, a region that includes New Zealand, Samoa, and Fiji. Island nations, such as the Maldives and places in the Caribbean Sea, and countries with many miles of coastline, including Iceland and Portugal, rely most heavily on fish.

Average Yearly Supply of Food Fish per Person

Less than 4.4 lb. (2 kg)	4.4–11 lb. (2–5 kg)	11–22 lb. (5–10 kg)	22–44 lb. (10–20 kg)	44–66 lb. (20–30 kg)	66–132 lb. (30–60 kg)	More than 132 lb. (60 kg)

A trawler sets out to sea off the coast of France.

CHAPTER 2

From the Wild

For hundreds of years, fishers have set out in boats or searched along coastlines for seafood such as fish and **shellfish**. Today, some of the seafood consumed is still caught in the wild. Fishing vessels include small boats that leave and return to port the same day. There are also giant factory ships capable of catching, processing, and freezing their catch. These huge ships can store thousands of pounds of frozen fish and may stay at sea for months.

 Oceans cover two-thirds of Earth's surface.

Longline Fishing

Many commercial, or business, fishers use longline fishing. This method is often used for tuna, salmon, cod, and other fish. The line is stored wrapped around a drum on the boat's deck. In the area the crew plans to fish, crew members unspool the line into the water. Some large boats carry lines 40 miles (64 kilometers) long. The main line has a series of smaller, branched lines. Each branch has a baited hook at the end.

A fisher unspools a longline into the water.

Depending on what type of fish they hope to catch, the fishers may use floating **buoys** to keep the line near the surface. This targets animals swimming near the water's surface. Fishers may also let the line drift to the seafloor to catch animals that swim

A fisher pulls in cod.

there. Either way, the crew activates the huge drums after a time to wind the line back onto the boat. As the line comes in, fish that have been hooked on the branched lines are brought on board.

Some fishing boats can release two nets at a time, one on each side.

Fishing With Nets

Some fishers use nets instead of lines. Large drift nets are allowed to drift near the surface of the water to catch fish swimming there. Boats may also drag a net to catch shellfish. Trawl nets often target a variety of fish or shrimp. These nets are huge and funnel-shaped. Sea life gets caught in the wide mouth of the net and becomes trapped.

Traps and Pots

Some sea animals, such as certain lobsters, crabs, and crawfish, are caught with traps. There are also traps designed for octopuses and eels. Traps are sometimes called pots. Fishers add bait before placing the traps in the water. Usually, the traps are attached to buoys so fishers can find their traps later. The next day, the fishers haul in the traps, gather their catch, add fresh bait, and put the traps back in the water.

People who catch lobsters are called lobstermen.

Seagulls flock around a fishing boat and its nets, hoping to grab some of the boat's catch.

Fishing Issues

Commercial fishing has risks. Bait may attract sharks, sea turtles, marine mammals, and fish that are either unwanted or too small. They can also become trapped in nets. These animals are called **bycatch**. Seabirds sometimes flock around longline boats to feed on the baited hooks and become tangled. In bottom trawling, the net drags along the seafloor. This can destroy plants, animals, and entire habitats on the seafloor, including coral reefs.

Ghost Nets

Sometimes a drift net snags on a reef or shipwreck and pulls free from a fishing boat. Fishers also occasionally discard old nets overboard deliberately. Whether freed by accident or on purpose, these nets are called ghost nets. They continue to trap and kill marine animals, and are among the biggest killers in our oceans. Some experts estimate that 100,000 marine mammals die each year due to ghost nets and other gear. Sea turtles and seabirds are also common victims.

A sea turtle caught in a ghost net

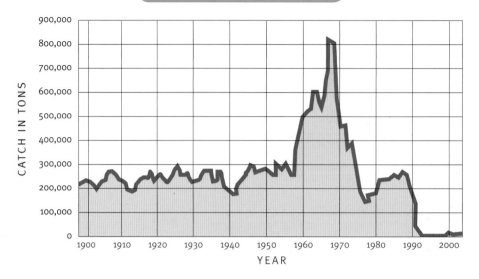

Atlantic Cod in Canada

Overfishing

Earth's oceans are so vast, it can seem as though there should be enough fish to last forever. Unfortunately, people catch some types of fish faster than new fish are born. As a result, wild populations decrease. Today, many species of fish are declining in numbers, and some are in real danger. By the mid-1900s, two popular food fish, Atlantic cod and California sardines, were on the brink of extinction as a result of overfishing.

Fish that are large, are slow to reproduce, or live a long time are most affected by overfishing. Orange roughy, bluefin tuna, and Chilean sea bass are examples. When large fish such as these disappear, fishers turn to smaller species such as sardines and squid. These species are important prey for larger fish, birds, and marine mammals. As a result, removing them from the food chain affects many other animals in the ocean **ecosystem**.

Orange roughy are caught faster than they can reproduce in the wild.

Running Out

Scientists predict that without action, all species of wild sea life we catch for food will disappear by 2050. Overfishing, pollution, climate change, and habitat destruction all contribute to this problem. These are just a few of the species that are most in danger of disappearing.

BLUEFIN TUNA
All three species of bluefin tuna are in danger of extinction. Bluefin tuna are a popular ingredient in sushi and sashimi, Japanese dishes. The fish is so popular that a bluefin can sell for more than $1,000 a pound ($450 per kilogram).

Bluefin Tuna

Orange Roughy

Atlantic Cod

Atlantic Salmon

ATLANTIC COD

Cod are used in many different ways, from cod-liver oil to fish and chips. Centuries of heavy fishing have caused populations of Atlantic cod in particular to fall dangerously low. In some areas, fishing cod is illegal. However, fishing in both legal and illegal areas has led to continued problems.

ORANGE ROUGHY

This fish only became a popular dish in recent decades. In that time, the population has dropped to a fraction of its original size. Orange roughy gather in groups, so fishers can catch them in huge volumes. The fish also reproduce slowly. New roughy are not born fast enough to replace all the adults that are caught.

ATLANTIC SALMON

Because of declining salmon populations, Atlantic salmon have been farmed since 1864. Heavy fishing continued, however. Today, so few Atlantic salmon are left that it is illegal for commercial fishers to target them.

Rows of enclosures are lined up in the water on a fish farm.

CHAPTER 3

Fish Farms

Before too long, it may not be possible to catch fish in the oceans. Species may disappear completely, or those that remain will be legally protected from continued fishing. But Earth's population is growing, and the demand for fish is increasing. Is there another way for us to obtain fish? Fish farming, or **aquaculture**, offers one possible alternative.

Some enclosures can hold hundreds of pounds worth of fish.

A Crop of Fish

Hatcheries are places that breed adult fish or shellfish and care for their eggs. After hatching, fish are moved to tanks or cages on a fish farm. Freshwater fish may be in a lake, pond, or river. Saltwater fish are kept in coastal ocean areas. Shellfish such as oysters and clams are usually raised in rivers or in coastal areas where the tide moves in and out. Mussels grow on ropes attached to rafts or the ocean bottom.

More than half the fish consumed worldwide are raised on fish farms.

A fish farmer scoops food pellets into a fish enclosure.

Feeding Farmed Fish

Like all farm animals, fish need to eat, and they eat a lot. What fish eat on a farm depends partly on what the species eats in the wild. Wild catfish, carp, and tilapia may eat insects or smaller fish, but they can also survive on plants. On farms, these fish are often fed pellets of corn, wheat, and other plants. This is cheaper and more efficient than a meat-based diet.

Carnivorous, or meat-eating, fish are another story. Tuna and salmon are the most common examples. Wild tuna and salmon eat smaller fish. On fish farms, they eat anchovies and herring, which are caught in the wild. They need a lot of this food. Tuna and salmon eat 5 pounds (2.3 kg) of food for every 1 pound (0.5 kg) they gain! As a result, such fish farms actually make the problem of overfishing worse.

Timeline of Aquaculture Developments

3500 BCE
The first recorded use of aquaculture occurs in China, where farmers raise carp.

2000 BCE
Japanese people begin to farm oysters.

1733 CE
A fish farmer in Germany raises fish from eggs to maturity for the first time.

Failures of Farming

Farmed fish live much closer together than wild fish. The dense collection of fish produces a lot of fish droppings that can pollute surrounding waters. There is also an increased risk of disease. Sea lice are **parasites** that attach to a fish's skin and spread easily among fish. Fish farmers usually treat affected fish with **antibiotics**. However antibiotics also spread into waterways and remain in the fish when they're sold.

1880s
People begin looking for ways to effectively farm lobster.

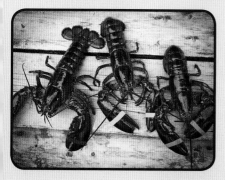

1960s
The first shrimp farms are established in Japan.

1999
For the first time, fish farmers produce more salmon than fishers catch in the wild.

Shrimp Farms

A particularly damaging example of aquaculture is shrimp farming. Many shrimp farms are built along coastlines, where farmers have cleared natural habitats such as mangrove forests. People and wildlife need these forests. Mangroves protect the coast from storm damage. They are also natural hatcheries for wild sea life. Waste and antibiotics from the shrimp farms can pollute the surrounding water and land. Some shrimp farms have had to be shut down because of disease.

The remains of a mangrove forest line a stream that runs through shrimp farms in Indonesia.

A New Kind of Salmon

A **genetically engineered** salmon may one day help farms produce salmon faster than ever. Genes influence how an animal looks and behaves. Scientists have altered the fish's genes so it reaches full size in only 20 months. Regular salmon take three years! Some people worry the altered fish could escape and compete with wild salmon for food. To prevent this, fish farmers will raise the fish in an enclosure on land. Scientists have also made sure the new salmon cannot reproduce or survive on their own.

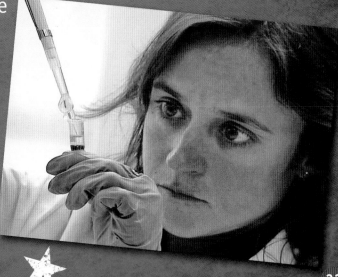

Fish form an important part of countless meals around the world.

CHAPTER 4

Better Methods

Whether we catch seafood in the wild or raise them on farms, we create problems for our oceans and the animals that live in them. Catching wild seafood reduces wild populations and can damage surrounding wildlife and habitats. Aquaculture can release pollutants or disease into the wild. As our global population grows, however, more fish will be needed. What's the solution? Should people stop eating fish? Or is there a better way to raise them?

World production of farm-raised fish is greater than world production of beef.

A Better Kind of Fish Farm

If we rely on fish farming, we will need to solve the many issues it presents. Many people are working on more environment-friendly, **sustainable** fish farm methods. Scientists have developed systems where fish are raised in huge tanks with solid walls. The tanks can either float in the ocean or operate entirely on land.

Fish swim through the clear waters of a sustainable fish farm in Italy.

The water in this fish farm pond will later be recycled and used to water the farmers' crops.

The water used in solid tanks is filtered to remove fish waste and recycled back through the tanks. This provides a constant supply of clean water, which reduces the spread of disease. And because the tanks are closed, water from the fish farm does not pollute the surrounding land or water. There are also no worries about fish escaping and affecting wild populations.

Another option is to locate fish farms far out in the open ocean. The strong, steady currents carry away fish waste and pests. Water temperature and the amount of salt in the water are more constant there than near land. This means the fish are less stressed and less likely to become sick.

These improvements should help farmers produce more and healthier fish. Such changes could protect wild species and provide food to the planet's many people. ★

A boat travels near fish enclosures in the Mediterranean Sea.

Frozen Fish

Fresh seafood spoils very quickly. Refrigerating seafood can extend its shelf life to a few days. Freezing, however, keeps seafood edible for months.

Frozen fish is most often cut into portions called fillets before being sold. It is sometimes cut into smaller portions to make fish sticks. Other seafood is processed similarly. Some, such as shrimp, might be frozen whole or cut to include only the edible portions.

SEAFOOD AND YOU!

Fish and other seafood are excellent sources of protein. Certain fish are also among the few sources of omega-3, a fat that keeps your heart healthy. However, be mindful of the seafood you and your family order at a restaurant or buy at the store. Here are some tips to keep in mind as you shop.

STICK TO SAFE SPECIES

Check out lists of fish and seafood that are good or bad for the environment. For example, catfish and king crab are good choices. But orange roughy and bluefin tuna should be avoided. Greenpeace's "Red List" and Monterey Bay Aquarium's "Seafood Watch" are great places to start. Ask an adult to help you find these lists online.

CHOOSE LOCAL

For wild-caught fish, your grocery store may have fish or seafood that were caught locally. However, most U.S. waters have been overfished, so local fish is not always available. Guides published online can offer recommendations depending on where you live. Ask an adult for help finding them.

WATCH THE MERCURY

Mercury is a substance that damages the brain and other parts of our nervous system. People can be exposed to mercury by eating certain fish. A good rule of thumb is to have no more than two meals of fish each week, and smaller fish and shellfish are better. Other fish, such as swordfish, marlin, and certain tunas, should be avoided completely. For more specific guidelines, there are lists online that detail which species are safest to eat. The U.S. Environmental Protection Agency and the Natural Resources Defense Council are good places to start. Ask an adult for help finding them.

Farmed or Wild-Caught?

Aquaculture is more popular today than ever, and it's still growing. However, the change from wild-caught to farmed fish is hotly debated. Some people argue that wild-caught fish are healthier both for the consumer and for the environment. Others believe aquaculture is the best way to feed a growing world population.

Which side do you agree with? Why?

Yes Keep eating wild-caught seafood!

As long as people are careful to avoid overfished species, wild-caught seafood is the better option. Aquaculture has a number of serious issues. **Some fish farms damage the local environment.** Shrimp farms have caused much of the world's loss of coastal mangrove forests. Badly designed farms may release fish waste and diseases, making wild populations sick. The farmed fish may also escape, if their enclosures are in water. Then they compete with wild populations for food. In addition, carnivorous farmed fish require a lot of food, which often consists of smaller fish taken from the wild.

Wild-caught fish may be healthier than farmed fish. Studies have found that wild fish have fewer chemicals that may cause cancer. They also are never treated with antibiotics, as some farmed fish are.

No Protect natural habitats!

Too many species are in danger of disappearing from overfishing. And as the world's human population grows, it will only put more pressure on wild fish and shellfish populations. Aquaculture can meet this demand while protecting wildlife.

Aquaculture practices are improving. **Researchers are developing more sustainable and more nutritious fish food for farms.** For example, protein-rich soybeans and other plants can replace the small fish used for feed. This means we don't have to catch those small fish in the wild. Algae is also being added to boost the feed's omega-3 content. This makes the farmed fish themselves more nutritious.

In addition, **designers are working on more efficient, more eco-friendly fish farms**. Some will be built inland, away from the water. Then the farmed fish could neither escape nor contaminate the water with their waste. Farms may also recycle their water, treating and cleaning it on-site.

Number of people around the world who rely on seafood as a major protein source: 1 billion

Amount of fish the average person worldwide eats per year: More than 44 lb. (20 kg)

Percent of the ocean affected by pollution and overfishing: 41

Amount of fish caught in the wild for human consumption each year: 65 million tons

Amount of wild-caught fish used for animal feed each year: 30 million tons

Percent of the world's fish habitats that are overfished or depleted: 32

Did you find the truth?

F All fish live on a plant-based diet.

T Fishers catch octopuses and eels using traps.

Resources

Book

Francine, Gabriella, and Solara Vayanian. *Let's Make a Difference: Learning About Our Ocean*. Newport Beach, CA: BBM Books, 2015.

Taylor-Butler, Christine. *Fish*. New York: Children's Press, 2014.

Visit this Scholastic Web site for more information about seafood:
★ www.factsfornow.scholastic.com
Enter the keyword **Seafood**

Important Words

antibiotics (an-ti-bye-AH-tiks) drugs that are used to kill bacteria and to treat infections and diseases

aquaculture (AH-kwuh-kuhl-chur) the cultivation of fish or shellfish, especially for food

buoys (BOO-eez) floating markers, often with a bell or light, that warn boats of underwater dangers or show them where to go

bycatch (BYE-katch) the portion of a commercial fishing catch that consists of animals caught unintentionally

ecosystem (EE-koh-sis-tuhm) all the living things in a place and their relation to their environment

genetically engineered (juh-NET-ihk-lee en-juh-NEERD) changed an organism's genes in order to produce a desired quality

parasites (PAR-uh-sites) animals or plants that live on or inside of another animal or plant

shellfish (SHEL-fish) creatures with shells that live in water, such as crabs, oysters, or mussels

sustainable (suh-STAY-nuh-buhl) done in a way that can be continued and that doesn't use up natural resources

Index

Page numbers in **bold** indicate illustrations.

About the Author

Ann O. Squire is a psychologist and an animal behaviorist. Before becoming a writer, she studied the behavior of rats, tropical fish in the Caribbean, and electric fish from central Africa. Her favorite part of being a writer is the chance to learn as much as she can about all sorts of topics. In addition to *Seafood* and other books in the Farm to Table series, Dr. Squire has written about many different animals, from lemmings to leopards and cicadas to cheetahs. She lives in Asheville, North Carolina.